THE ALL NEW STYLE OF MAGAZINE-BOOKS

SDM

www.SDMLIVE.com

MP

MOCY PUBLISHING
WWW.MOCYPUBLISHING.COM

Printed by CreateSpace, An Amazon.com Company

SDM

EDITOR-IN-CHIEF
D. "Casino" Bailey
casino@sdmlive.com

EDITORIAL DIRECTOR
Sheree Cranford
sheree@sdmlive.com

GRAPHIC/WEB DESIGNER
D. "Casino" Bailey
casino@sdmlive.com

A&R MANAGER
Aye Money
ayemoney@sdmlive.com

ACCOUNT EXECUTIVE
Frank Harvest Jr.
frank@sdmlive.com

PHOTOGRAPHERS
Treagen Colston
D. "Casino" Bailey

CONTRIBUTORS
Minyetta Nelson
Courtney Benjamin

COPY ORDERS & ADVERTISING OFFICE
Send Money Order or Check to:
Mocy Publishing
P.O. Box 35195
Detroit, Michigan 48235
(586) 646-8505
advertise@sdmlive.com

Copy Order Item #:
SDM Magazine Issue #11 2016
S&H Plus Retail Price - $9.99 per copy

WWW.SDMLIVE.COM

Printed by CreateSpace, An Amazon.com Company

MP
MOCY PUBLISHING

Copyright © 2016 Support Detroit Movement,
a division of Aye Money Promotions & Publishing, LLC and
Mocy Music Publishing, LLC. All rights reserved.
Printed in the U.S.A.

REAL MUSIC. REAL ENTERTAINMENT.

SDM

ISSUE 11

TEAM MONEY HUNGRY

VERZELL

CRIMSON ALCHEMIST

KING27

GREG G-ROCK SANDERS

3XOTIC

BRIAN JONES

DJ HOLLYHOOD
AN INTERNATIONAL DJ WITH DETROIT SWAGG

TEAM MONEY HUNGRY GETTING READY FOR THE NEW YEAR WITH NEW MUSIC & VIDEOS

CONTENTS

1

Wireless Bluetooth FM Transmitter Radio Adapter Receiver, CHGeek 3.4A Dual USB Car Charger with Hands-free Calling Supports USB Flash Drive
$33.99
www.amazon.com

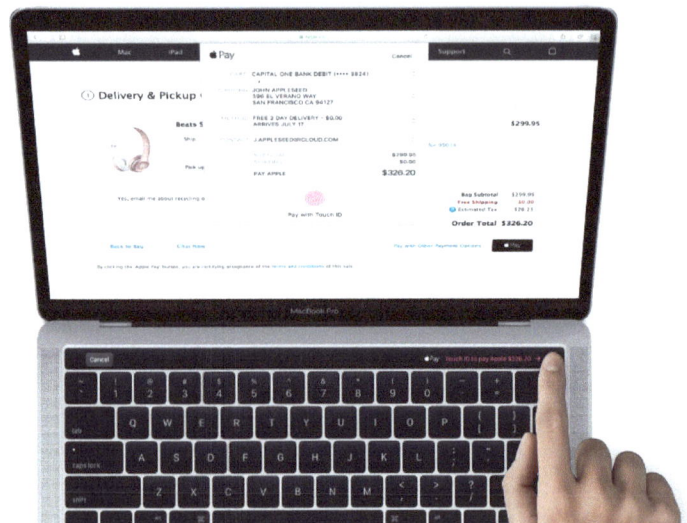

2

Amazon Echo - Black
$179.99
www.amazon.com

3

New Apple 13 Inch MacBook Pro / MD101LL/A / 2.5GHz Intel Core i5, 4GB RAM, 500GB HDD, DVDRW, Intel HD 4000 Graphics
$867.59
www.amazon.com

Key's Slays Naturally

CAN WOMEN LIVE IN A WORLD WITHOUT MAKEUP FILTERS OR IS CONTOURING AND BLENDING MAC AND COVERGIRL ALL A WOMAN KNOWS?

by Cheraee C.

Singer and feminist Alicia Keys has started a powerful and emotional no makeup movement. Keys has shown light on her own inner shallowness and intends to empower women all over the world with her bare, basic face. She doesn't want to let fame, society, the paparazzi, the media or etc no longer dictate when or if a woman should publicly wear makeup.

Makeup is widely and insecurely viewed as an necessity, when it should be viewed as an on and off accessory. It's women who will not leave the house without putting some type of makeup on their face. It's nothing wrong with having a polished look, but women are becoming the makeup. Women are masking themselves, their blemishes, their pain, and their real insecurities. Some women aren't happy with the color of their skin, their own birthmarks, scars, stretch marks, their bra sizes, their waist sizes, and the problem goes even deeper. As long as society keeps making products that help women conceal themselves, and their flaws, women will never define their confidence. Instead their confidence

will continue to be defined by America. The traditional woman is natural from her head to her feet, and is confident in herself and her culture. The traditional woman speaks, dresses, and walks with class and dignity. Yet today's women let society declare what is fashionable, walk with facades, and speak ghetto and ignorantly like they don't have a vocabulary. Women have lost a sense of substance and a sense of their roots.

All of Mrs. Keys recent public appearances whether she has to slay a red carpet or not, have all been done without makeup. Some critics have been bashing and ridiculing Alicia for not wearing makeup publicly, like Alicia can't be her own woman. Like Alicia Keys isn't just one woman, who just so happens to be makeupless compared to all the millions of other women in the world still wearing makeup like a day job. Society must be afraid that America will soon begin to idolize her for not wearing makeup, and follow suit.

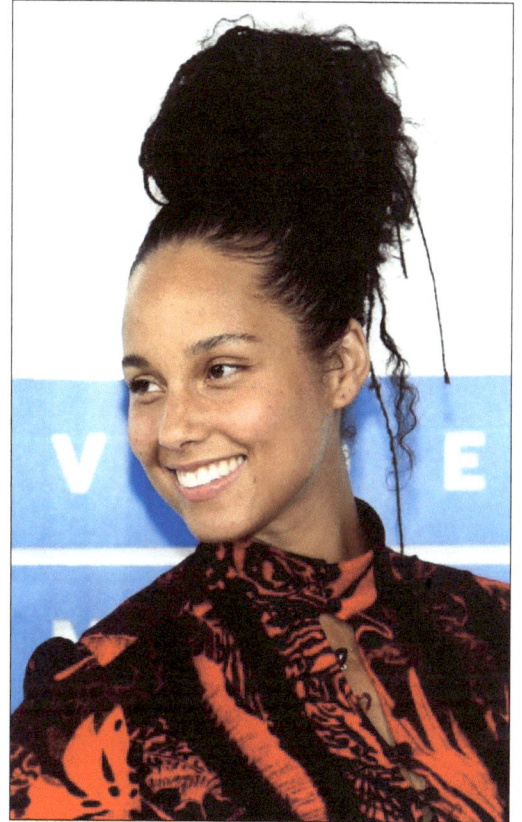

Patience is a Virtue

THE DYNAMIC COUPLE MEAGAN GOOD AND DEVON FRANKLIN EMPOWER THE WORLD SHARING THEIR STORY OF WAITING

by Cheraee C.

Some people are new school and pick and choose what beliefs they choose to enhance their relationship with or without. Some people don't have marriage as a short or long term goal in their relationship, and are copacetic with just being boyfriend and girlfriend. While some people are traditional and still believe in celibacy and marriage. Meagan Good and DeVon Franklin are a prime example.

Even though they are rich and famous, doesn't exempt them from a constant issue a lot of people have which is finding the one. Why rush into being in a relationship, when you can genuinely take your time? A relationship is built on time anyway, and their book gives you a look at how they waited for each other and gives you tips on how you can practice waiting for you soulmate.

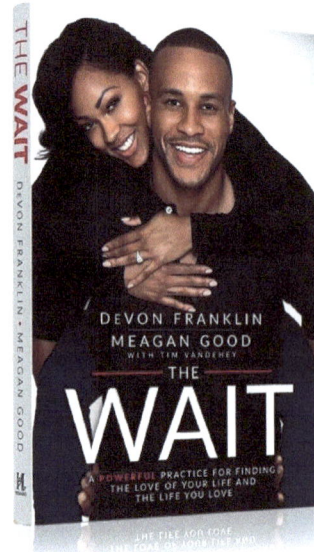

The Wait
By DeVon Franklin

Available from Amazon.com and other online stores

TOP 10 COUNTDOWN
MUSIC VIDEOS
FRIDAYS & SATURDAYS
9PM EST

Hosted by
BINO THE
PERSONALITY

SDM on ROKU TV

Go DJ, That's My DJ

SOUTHWEST DJ HOLLYHOOD DOESN'T NEED TO JOIN A MOVEMENT BECAUSE HE'S A MOVEMENT BY HIMSELF AND HIS NETWORK IS IN FULL EXPANSION MODE
by Cheraee C.

Q. How long have you been deejaying and what legendary DJ's do you idolize in Michigan and outside of Michigan?
A. I've been deejaying since 2008 and growing up in southwest Detroit. I used to be amazed by DJ Waxtax and Dre. The mixtapes he sed to make was cold and I had to have every one soon as they hit the local reecord store in southwest. DJ Clue was my favorite out of town DJ. His mixtapes had me hooked on just listening to freestyles and diss tracks.

Q. How do you feel about the current Detroit DJ movements such as the Coalition DJ's and Street Hitta DJ's? Are you apart of any of these movements or are you solo dolo and why?
A. I really don't know much about those dj groups except for them having some great dj's in them. There was talks of me joining one of them, but I guess I didn't make the cut lol.

Q. If you had an event with DJ Khalid, DJ Drama, or DJ Quik, who would yo choose to dj with and why?
A. Wow, this is a tough one lol as bad as I wanna pick DJ Quik i'm going to go with DJ Khalid because I've seen him make a stadium go crazy and the major artists, and the hot singles that come with him. Shows would definitely be crazy. Lol, my people are gonna kill me for choosing Khalid over Quik.

Q. What types of events do you dj at the most and are there any types of events you don't dj at?
A. I mostly dj weddings, baby showers, and concerts. Weddings are my favorite events though because I love the full-room dj setups, the lights, and all the wedding formalities that go with it. I stay away from strip clubs, and bars. No reason in particular I just really like working halls where I can showcase my dj setups.

Q. How do you deal with crazy event planners and wedding planners and what is the worst deejaying experience you've had at an event?
A. I try to ignore crazy event planners lol, but it never works. They always end up getting under my skin. The worst thing to ever happen at a gig was people bringing outside liquor in a hall that had a bar, and the hall staff shut down the whole thing and ended the party.

Q. When your dealing with guests at an event and their music requests, how do you handle guests who request lame music?

DJ Hollyhood

A. Lame music requests are the worst lol. I've had people try to tip me to play songs that might get me yelled at by my client lol. I try to ignore them or tell them I don't have the song, and no internet to download it.

Q. How do you feel about all the rap drama going on between Big Gov, JP One, or any Detroit rap artists
currently fueding?

A. I met Gov around 96 or 97. We went to the same high school and ended up with the same lunch hour and I would always bring my brush to lunch so I could make beats on the table and he was always the first one to drop a freestyle. I wasn't added to the team until 2012. I hate the beef/drama because I'm good friends with both of them even with them having the most entertaining weekend for two rappers dropping songs in Detroit this year. I want to see it end. I definitely don't like seeing two of my friends on a collision course. I often sit and think about all the great music that we are missing out on with them not working together anymore. I haven't seen any other local fueds lately. I think for the most part, the city has been starting to come together.

Q. What types of characteristics does a song have to have as far as a diss track or new, underground music for you to spin their record at an event?

A. Unless I'm at an album release party where I'm forced to play a diss song, I'm not playing it. As far as playing underground music at gigs, I always find a way to drop some new songs at my events. As a DJ, I feel it's my responsibility to get unheard music out there whenever I can and I request music from artists I see putting in work all the time.

The Cosmos of Music & Gorillas

MUSICIAN AND COSMIC CREATOR GREG G-ROCK SANDERS GIVES THE 411 ON HIS ALBUM, HIS BAND, AND HIS TV SERIES COMING TO SDM NETWORK

by: Cheraee C.

Q. Tell us three personal things about yourself most people don't know about you?

A. Well nothing really special comes to mind except that I'm pretty much a visionary meaning and everything I do comes from a visual standpoint. I write music with a picture and a certain emotion that I'm trying to portray. I care deeply about our people and want to uplift our youth to greatness whenever I get the chance...I'm a multi-instrumentalist playing bass, lead guitar, and keyboards. I'm also a prolific songwriter able to cross many genres..

Q. Who started Gorilla Funk Mob (band) and how did you become apart of it?

A. Gorilla Funk Mob was formed by myself and Drummer Tate McBroom. I came up with the name and he helped with bookings and management. We started in the early 2000s as a band that would play behind a variety of artists in different genres eventually becoming known as the premier hip-hop band of Detroit. We played behind artists including S.U.N., Phat Katt, Slum Village, Finale Supa MC., Paradime Danny Brown, and recently SDM's own Pamela P-Dot Willis. But now we have finally took a break and written and recorded a groundbreaking new cd with our new line up that includes James Shelton on keyboards ,Josh Meyer on guitar, and reknowned Detroit vocalist and artist Pierre Anthony, myself, and Tate McBroom.

Q. What is the Galactic Gorilla and The Cosmic Brotherhood? What made you want to venture into animated cartoons?

A. This is something I've been thinking about and creating in my head for a few years. It's a out of the box space graphic comic from a minority standpoint where I have a character named High Commander G-Rock and my mentor is a gorilla named Galactic and we formed a sort of space military force called the Cosmic Brotherhood. We defend the galaxy mainly from a super villian and his minions named the Red Menace and believe me the story lines are bananas as intended. I ventured into it because I love comics and also i want minority youth to see that there is many other things they can do besides rap or sports. They can become the next Stan Lee or whatever I mean they can be anything they can visualize so I wanted to make it as unusual as I could.

Q. You seem to be fascinated with gorillas because you have Gorilla Funk Mob and The Galactic Gorilla cartoon you created. Why are gorillas so symbolic to you?

A. Well I've always been fascinated by gorillas they are pure noble strong animals who unlike man are custodians of the Earth. They eat the fruits and what's avaliable in the jungle and recycle it right back in the environment replenishing the jungle. I watched a special on Koko, the gorilla, and she knows sign language. She said in sign language that she loves man, but we are running out of time to save the Earth from our pollution and man-made destruction that stuck out in my mind. I started saying to myself, what if a gorilla played music? He would be free of constraints in styles of funk jazz what have ya and he would play whatever he felt with ferociousness. So I came up with Gorilla Funk and put that philosophy in the forefront.

Q. Tell us about your CD Back To Bassix. Is that the first CD you released as an artist, and what is your favorite song on that album and why?

A. My CD Back To Bassix is my first solo bass venture as an artist. I have plenty much just been a work horse musically touring, producing, and recording for numerous artists along with my good friend Tony Ozier who helped me as an engineer and producer. We recorded this blend of instrumental funk jazz fusion and some neo soul r&b tracks really spotlighting my bass playing. My favorite song on the CD would be Pimpalicious because it's purely vicious and you can buy the cd @www.Longrangedistribution.com code letter G. I usually have CD's at our live shows also.

Q. How do you feel about the SDM movement and what are your future plans to collaborate with SDM?

A. I am very excited about the SDM movement. I really like your format with Roku and the variety of shows I've seen, and the magazine on top of that. It's deemed to really be a good platform for Detroit artists and to have my comic on the roster, I would love to grow and expand my audience with y'all help. I see great things for the network and I am happy to get a chance to grow with you guys.

Experience Verzell

COMPOSER, MUSICIAN, AND SINGER VERZELL IS READY TO REDEFINE THE MUSIC INDUSTRY FROM LACKING SUBSTANCE AND TRUE ARTISTRY
by Cheraee C.

Q. Do you feel like music is finding its way back to it's more traditional and sensational roots or is it becoming more and more materialistic and unrealistic?

A. I feel as though music is moving further into materialism, mainstream music in particular. The commerical push of music that lacks substance has dulled the listener's ear. This creates a void I intend on filling. Bringing it back down to the roots where if you were an entertainer,, you had to write your music, sing your music, and play your music. All of which God has blessed me to do (sing, write, and play instruments.)

Q. Who was the first major producer or mentor you worked with in the music industry and describe that experience?

A. I've worked with producer D Digital, who's produced for acts like Day 26, Tiffany Evans, Fetty Wap, and more. D Digital produced a song on my upcoming project and the song is called Cest La Vie. As a musician, I notice the difference between a beatmaker and a producer. D Digital is defintely a "producer" who caters to bring out the sound in an artist. In terms of mentorship, Brandon Smith of Star Factory taught me alot about the industry. He also developed my gifts as a teen, as Star Factroy is a talent development agency. He developed my knowledge of industry as well as marketing, branding, contracts, and etc.

Q. What are some of the things you do before a performance or a studio session to prepare? Is it a certain tune you practice? Do you fast? Do you take a shot or etc?

A. Before a performance, I'm generally alone in the corner having a glass of wine, meditating on my show. Every show has a different energy so I take in the environment before I execute.

Q. What is your opinion of the lyrics that come from mainstream and underground singers? Whick lyrics lack substance? Which lyrics are setting trends?

A.The lyrics are far too basic, and leaves little room for imagination. It's okay to have those songs "sometimes" but not all the time. Even I'm guilty of perhaps 1-2 basic songs out of a collection. But even in those circumstances there should be a clear message. Put it this way, Stevie Wonder's commercial hit back in the day, which prompted the Electric Slide. It started out with the lyrics, "I was a lonely no one living in the vacuum of life's debris," deep isn't it? Of today's music, I have to respect Frank Ocean and Miguel as songwriters. there is a select few of us that still strive to challenge the minds through words. My debut single "Love is Like a Drug" captures that concept filled with triple meanings and metaphors. The lyricism is the key component in that song, and why it was important for me to lead with that single. I wanted my fans to feel my music, as our parents once had.

Q. A lot of artists are independent. What made you seek Loyalty Management and how do you feel about your current manager Teyuana Jackson?

A. I sought management because as an artist, independent or signed, you need a team to manage your affairs. That means lawyers to look over contracts, a booking agent, a good promo team etc. I found that I couldn't focus on my craft while wearing 1000 hats. It would take a person like me a million years to get things done haha. I sought a manager I can trust and handle dual roles. I feel thus far my manager has been effective in my career, and we have the common goal of reaching new heights. At the end of the day, it's about trust, and I completely trust Loyalty Ent.

A R&B and Rap Mix Breed

KING27 IS A MIXTURE OF USHER AND UNCLE LUKE AND HIS CURRENT CLUB BANGER "DROP THAT" GOT THE STREETS SIZZLING AND TWERKING

by Cheraee C.

Q. How long have you been grinding in the music industry and how would you describe yourself as an artist?

A. I have been grinding in the music industry for the past four years and I would describe myself and music as the modern day Usher and Uncle Luke. The reason I say that is because I am always told I remind people of them. The funny part is I grew up listening to them. Anytime I write a hype song it sounds like Uncle Luke most definitely when I am rapping.

Q. Tell us more about your music sides and exactly why your fans compare you to be a mix of Usher and Uncle Luke.

A. When I perform my single "Drop That" it's butt-shaking everywhere lol and if you ever see me perform, you will see I am a Jr. Uncle Luke and it goes down lol. On the other hand, I have a grown and sexy side of me which is the guy who can dance and sing, but when I sing and dance it's very smooth. Ladies say when I perform my love-making music and I dance with them it reminds them of Usher and they love it. That side of me is for women. I love them for that one night. I make them feel good inside and out with my moves and voice and I cater to they're needs. I become everything they want they're man to be. They walk to my shows ready and wanting more.

Q. Describe how you feel when your in your zone on stage performing.

A. Before walking on stage I am just Frederick Watts, but when my feet touch down, seems like everything changes. Once I get the vibe from the crowd, I forget what I was nervous about. I sometimes don't remember what I've done on stage til I get off and my camera man plays back my performance. And it's like wow, I did that. She said that, she touched me there wow, she let me do that to her lol. When I am in my zone I am in complete control, and no one can bring my high down.

Q. How do you maintain your composure in the spotlight, and have you ever felt starstruck?

A. I maintain my composure by keeping a positive circle, always staying positive and humble, and enjoying my surroundings. I have never been starstruck. I feel every star is just a normal person and is the same person they were before they became something great.

Q. Are you more focused on becoming a signed artist to a major label or becoming a CEO signing artists?

A. I am not really focused on becoming a signed artist to a major label because I deeply believe I can accomplish more on my own. I feel like at this point a major label cannot do anything for me besides take money out my pocket to help me out a little more. I wouldn't need anything, but that. I own my own label FMF Records and I am my only signed artist. I am more focused on me and my brand before focusing on someone else's brand. I would like to sign to a major label only if its through distribution, and I own my own publishings, masters, and names. Also, if I can control how I move and do what I want to do and I have a partnership percentage or more than I am all for it. I feel like I've reached a great point in my career right now that I should have great offers. Otherwise, I don't mind slamming the door on trash contracts.

The Industry's Best

THE TOP 12 MUSIC SCHOOLS OF MUSIC'S NEXT GENERATION

by Semaja Turner

The next generation of musical scholars, executives, artists, CEO's, composers, and etc are learning the music business at the top 12 music schools in the U.S.

1. Belmont University
The Mike Curb College of Entertainment and Music Business, Nashville, TN
2. Berklee College of Music, Boston, MA
3. Hofstra University, Hempstead, NY
4. Indiana University
Jacobs School of Music, Bloomington, IN
5. Middle Tennessee State University
School of Music, Murfreesboro, TN
6. New York University
Clive Davis Institute of Recorded Music, New York, NY
7. New York University
Stern School of Business, New York, NY
8. Syracuse University
Setnor School of Music, Syracuse, NY
9. University of California Los Angeles
Herb Alpert School of Music, Los Angeles, CA
10. University of Miami
Frost School of Music, Coral Gables, FL
11. University of Southern California
Jimmy Lovine and Andre Young Academy, Los Angeles, CA
12. University of Southern California
USC Thorton School of Music, Los Angeles, CA

Financial District

Hungry in The Streets

BLACK RAIN, WOODROW THE ENTERTAINER, MONTE SS, PRINCEAUHMAZIN, AND MANDY BABY ARE TAKING OVER THE STREETS LIKE CASH MONEY

by Cheraee C.

Q. Who are all the members of Team Money Hungry and is TMH a closed or open group?

A. TeamMoneyHungry consists of Black Rain, Woodrow the Entertainer, Monte SS, Princeauhmazin, and the newest member Mandy Baby on Fire. TMH started off with Black Rain as the only artist... and Donna Banks as the manager, but has grown to a multitude of members, fans, and supporters. TMH is an open group and we are recruiting people to become a part of the movement EVERYDAY!

Q. What awards were TMH nominated for at the 2016 Detroit Honor Awards and what was y'all best award moment that night?

A. Thee BIGGEST moment of the night was TMH accepting the trophy for all the hard work and dedication to our love for music! And right after accepting the award being able to perform and ignite the crowd with our energetic performance!

Q. It's plenty of big, show-stopping award shows. If TMH could open up for a major award show, which one would it be and why?

A. I would say the Grammy's. The reason being as a child, you looked forward to watching the Grammy's to see who would be considered the best of the best in the music industry, So to open up for the Grammy's and showcase our talent for the WORLD to see would be electrifying!!!

Q. TMH is a movement, you guys are everywhere. Who's idea was it to start TMH, and who keeps TMH together and relevant?

A. Michael "Black Rain" Flowers, this was his vision, to have a team of musical artists that can give the people music that they can enjoy, dance and party to. TMH was a dream initially, but now it has become all of our vision. At TMH we keep each other motivated. We strive on giving the people good quality music. Our supporters of the movement is what keeps us inspired.

Q. TMH is straight fire. When are y'all goin release an album, or a mixtape? What's y'all next power move?

A. A team album is going to come along down the line. We are in the works of a mixtape and we are about halfway there. We are focused on creating more team songs that highlight our brand and unique styles. TMH is committed to the ideal of entrepreneurship. Hardwork, dedication, internal motivation, and perseverance will make all of our moves powerful. The next step is branching out to different states and build-

ing a worldwide network. TMH is in the works of a really big project, something that will showcase our artistry on another level. Just stay tuned.. #TeamMoneyHungry is definitely on the move!

Unity is Priceless

THE CEO OF UNIFIED MUSIC & FILMS NETWORK BRIAN JONES IS ON A MISSION TO UNIFY THE MUSIC INDUSTRY BEGINNING WITH DETROIT

by Cheraee C.

Q. Describe your experience as an executive producer and what made you start ibelieverecords inc?

A. I've had several artists from 2005 until now under Bubble Dog Records. When my artist Mich E Mich died from a fatal car accident, I left that label and started ibelieverecords because I believe in the artist and I bring the best out of their artistry especially undiscovered artists.

Q. Describe the song you made that was featured on Channel 7 news and what inspired that story and song?

A. The song "My City" was made and recorded back in 2011. It features 10 artists that include Rell Devine, Malik, Byrd, Stretch Money, Jujitta, Lady Te, Helluva, and David Billy. Each artists uses their unique lyric styles so everyone can have a say and an imput about Detroit. Channel 7 was moved by my movement to reunify Detroit, especially as it relates to its music industry. It's crazy because the music industry is still as segregated as it was back in 2011.

Q. How did you meet Stretch Money, and what work did you do with him?

A. I've been knowing Stretch Money for years through Crane Novacane who I knew from both Bubble Dog Records and my eastside ties. After the song My City was recorded, I limoed everyone to my house in Novi and treated everyone to dinner, and DJ Snook and Doc FM had a show called the Late Night Special so I had them interview Stretch Money in my theatre room, and several other artists music interviews as well.

Q. Describe your relationship with Shawty Lo and how his death affected you?

A. I was introduced to Shawty Lo through my daughter's side of the family. One day he was in Downtown Detroit and I went to go meet him and we connected. He's a good guy and we were going to put on a big unity project to do music from the north and the south. His death was a shock to me.

Q. Who are the key players apart of the Unified Music& Film Movement besides yourself?

A. Kwasi Ware, COO of UMFN/BMG Management, D. Casino Bailey, CEO of UMFN/SDMNetwork, Maxwell Minks, President of UMFN/Alphawolf Re-

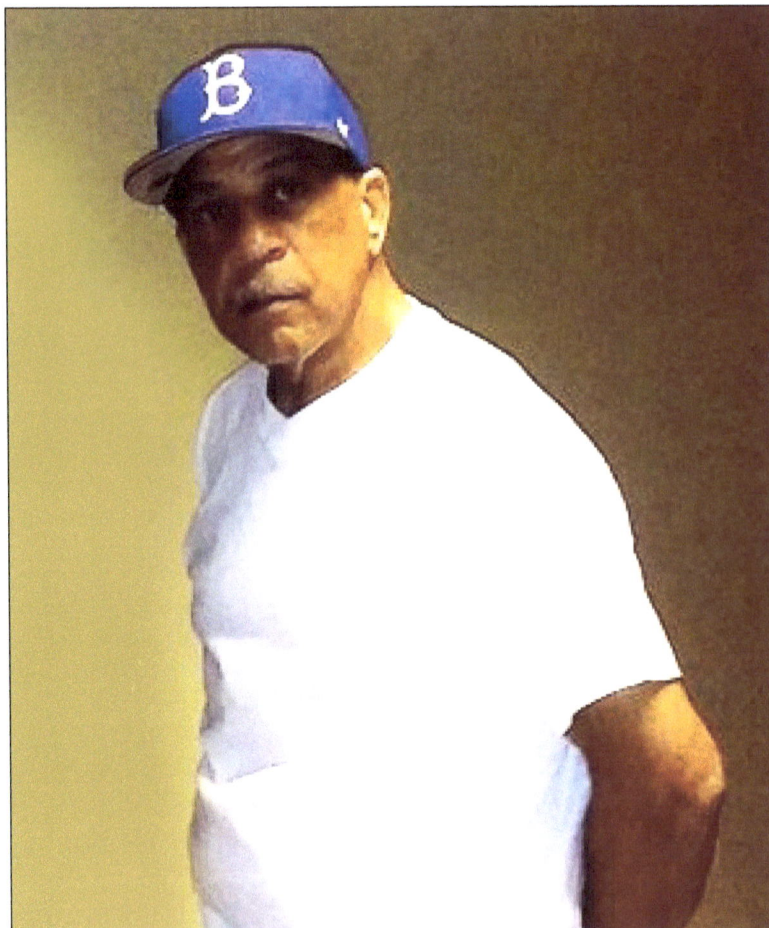

cords, Kelly Durden, Vice President of UMFN/Aye Money Promotions, Minyetta Nelson, Treasury of UMFN, and Barbara Redes, Secretary of UMFN.

Q. You mentioned to me about your vision in relationship to your city. I know that it's more to the song so how else do you plan to spread your message through the music business?

A. I've never seen anyone bring together a business such as mine Unified Music & Film Network with five different families. We are all in business together at our brand new building on the corner of Grand River and Greenfield. I'm going to start working on the film "My City" in early 2017. God told me to do music for the rest of my life so that's exactly what I'm going to do.

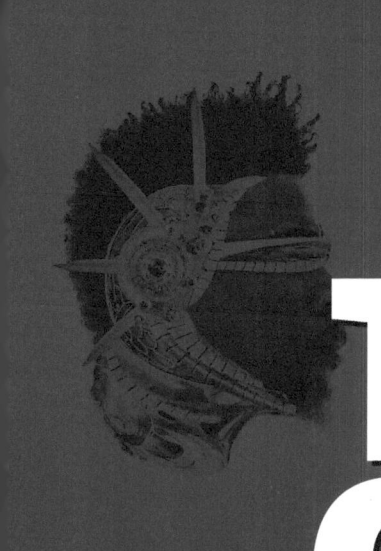

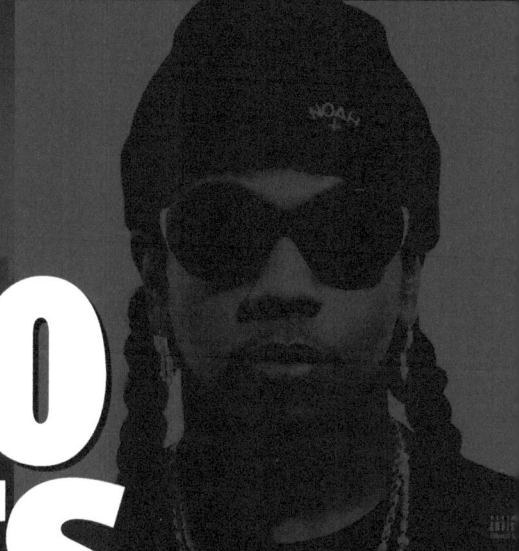

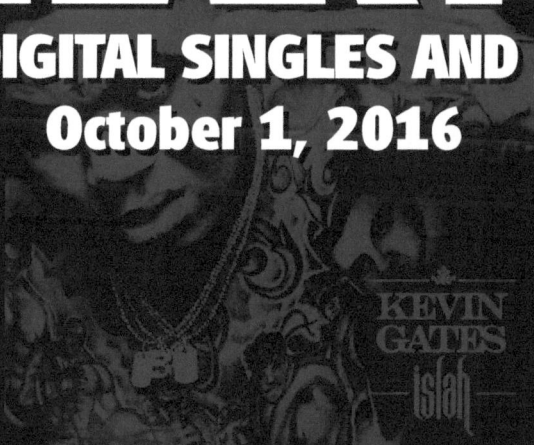
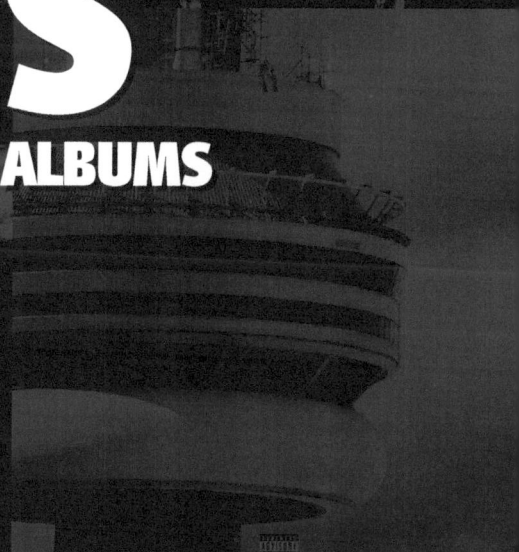

TOP 10 CHARTS

TOP 10 DIGITAL SINGLES AND ALBUMS
October 1, 2016

TOP 10 CHARTS

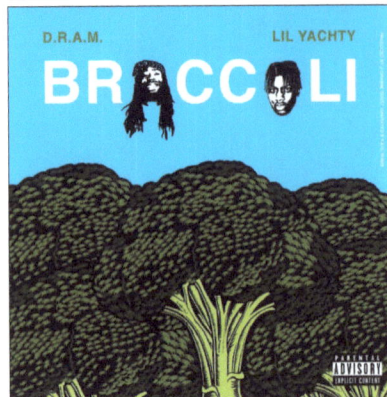

D.R.A.M.

Broccoli

Coming in at #1 this month, The trap song Broccoli has been certified 2x Platinum by the RIAA.

RAPPER LIL WAYNE ON THE SET OF HIS NEW VIDEO "SUCKER FOR PAIN".

TOP 10 SINGLES CHART OF THE MONTH

No.	Artist - Song Title
1	D.R.A.M. - BROCCOLI FT. LIL YACHTY
2	THE WEEKND - STARBOY FT DAFT PUNK
3	LIL WAYNE - SUCKER FOR PAIN
4	YOUNG MA - OOOUUU
5	BEYONCE - HOLD UP
6	TORY LANEZ - LUV
7	DJ KHALED - DO YOU MIND
8	KANYE WEST - FADE
9	KEHLANI - CRZY
10	SOLANGE - CRANES IN THE SKY

TOP 10 ALBUMS CHART OF THE MONTH

No.	Artist - Album Title
1	USHER - HARD II LOVE
2	TY DOLLA SIGN - CAMPAIGN
3	FRANK OCEAN - BLONDE
4	DJ KHALID - MAJOR KEY
5	DANNY BROWN - ATROCITY EXHIBITION
6	MAC MILLER - THE DIVINE FEMININE
7	MAXWELL - BLACKSUMMERS'NIGHT
8	TI - US OR ELSE (EP)
9	TORY LANEZ - I TOLD YOU
10	GUCCI MANE - EVERYBODY LOOKING

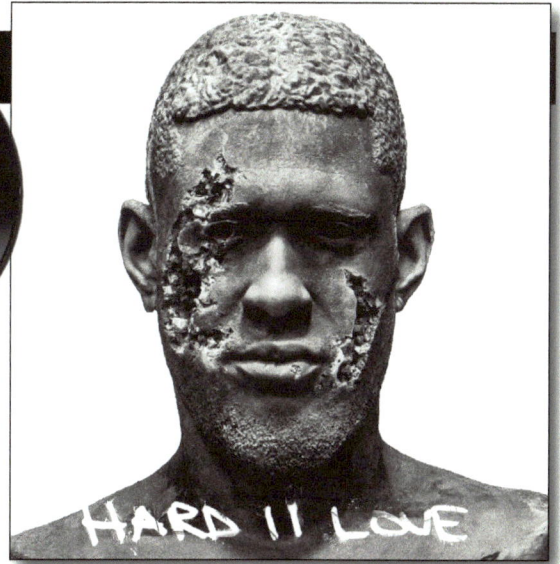

Hard II Love

ARTIST: Usher
REVIEWER: Cheraee C.
RATING: 2

If this album wasn't made by Usher, it prolly wouldn't be so popular. The music was typical Usher Raymond who keeps you in your feelings, but next album Usher needs to step outside the box and embark on a feeling other then love.

Singles from the album include No Limit featuring Young Thug, Champions with Ruben Blades, Need U featuring Priyanka Chopra, Make You A Believer, Mind Of A Man, and many other singles. I give this album two stars.

RATE METER: 1 - WACK   2 - NEEDS WORK   3 - STRAIGHT   4 - BANGER   5 - CLASSIC

Campaign

ARTIST: Ty Dolla Sign
REVIEWER: Cheraee C.
RATING: 5

Ty Dolla Sign makes nine seem like a charm, as he releases his ninth album full of dope music. With singles including Zaddy, Campaign featuring Future, Pu$$y featuring Trey Songs and Wiz Khalifa, $, Juice, My Song featuring 24hrs, Hello, Watching featuring Meek Mill, and many more. I give this album five stars.

Blonde

ARTIST: Frank Ocean
REVIEWER: Cheraee C.
RATING: 5

Mr. Ocean has been M.I.A. from the industry for seven years, but he's back with some classic music. Singles from the album include Pink+White featuring Beyonce, Skyline To featuring Kendrick Lamar, Solo (Reprise) featuring Andre 3000, Pretty Sweet, Good Guy, and more. I give this album five stars.

HEELS &
SKILLZ

Honey Da Truth

is a full-time model from Detroit, MI.

instagram
@honeydatruth

Photography by
@barearmy

HEELS &
SKILLZ

Meme
is a beautiful model
from Detroit, MI.

instagram
@alwaysmsme

Photography by
@dariusblackmon

HEELS &
SKILLZ

Hater Maker
is a sexy model
for barearmy and
lives in Detroit, MI.

facebook
@hatermaker313

Photography by
@barearmy

Cheraee's Corner
IS IT MORE BLACK ON BLACK CRIME OR WHITE ON BLACK CRIME?
by Cheraee C.

As widely used and viewed as the Black Lives Matter campaign is you would think that blacks and minorities would be upholding black lives and all lives to the fullest extent. Instead blacks continue on killing the black minority like it's an occupation with a 401K and full benefits. Then minorities are single-handedly killing the black minority using their race as leverage over the judicial system because the judicial system doesn't prosecute whites like they prosecute blacks.

There is no comparison on who is killing the black minority more or less. The fact that this unlawful and sporadic killing continues to occur should be the real issue. Why aren't people afraid to commit murder anymore and why is society entertaining the careless purging of innocent lives? Even though we are reposting and sharing videos of discrimination, having protests around our neighborhoods, and saying black lives matter, what is that really solving?

The whole world needs to be on one accord, so the focal point needs to change because black lives aren't the only lives that matter and almost every race has had their share of brutality. If we learn how to use the news, headlines, murders, beefs, and etc in positive ways then maybe we could generate change, and change the judicial system. It's like society has ADHD because the only thing that keeps our attention is anything that inflicts negativity. We've got to snap out of the blurs we are in and whip this society back into shape, before there is no society left.

NEXT 2 BLOW

CRIMSON ALCHEMIST

Q. Why do you call yourself the Crimson Alchemist?

A. I call myself the Crimson Alchemist because of the way I break every single bar down so that each one hits with a clever metaphor the average person wouldn't think of and red is my favorite color.

Q. What's the inspiration behind your new mixtape Vantablack and what can your fans look forward to with this EP?

A. The inspiration behind Vantablack is really just the trials and errors I've been going through with everyday life issues and obstacles that i've faced as I get further into the music industry. I want to get more personal with this EP. It just might be someone out there going thourgh the same thing that needs to hear it.

Q. Do you feel like female MC's are taken for granted in the music industry or that female MC's are starting to become less common and more respected?

A.Absolutely. There's so many here in Detroit alone that deserve the same amount of exposure as guys. If you're not rapping provocatively, sad to say, I tell people all the time that female emcees aren't scarce at all. We're hidden all over doing small open mics and poetry slams. If given a bigger platform, and an actual chance, more and more female emcees would gain the courage to come out and display their talent.

Q. You definitely have your own swag. How do you feel about Alicia Key's no make-up movement and how society tries to depict the cosmetic attributes of a woman in the public eye?

A. Thank you! I fully support Alicia Key's no makeup movement. Although, there are some people that are taking her movement the wrong way, as if she's anti makeup, which isn't the case at all. She's simply making a statement that there's nothing wrong with loving your skin for what it is. Each day women are put under the impression that we have to be a certain size and have flawless skin to be considered beautiful. That stretch marks and blemishes aren't appealing to the eye. With Alicia Keys' doing this, she's showing that it's okay to embrace your flaws. Anything that helps the empowerment of women, I'm here for it.

Q. *Just recently, Alicia Keys was being shamed for her no makeup movement. How do you feel about the way female artists struggle to be what society thinks is beautiful?*

A. I feel we should embrace different faces of beauty in this industry. Me being a plus sized artist, I get criticized a lot, but the good thing about having talent is sometimes what society thinks doesn't stand a chance. I feel there isn't a label on beauty, and the industry should be more open to different shades, shapes, and faces, and being comfortable with the skin you're in. That is what makes an artist unique.

Q. Who is your favorite plus-sized artist and how do you feel about the evolution of plus-sized artists once they hit the industry? Plus-sized one day and skinny the next.

A. I actually like all of them far as talent wise and opening up a new lane in the industry for plus-sized mainstream artists. As far as being plus-sized then skinny next, I feel it's nothing wrong with being healthier. But then you have women that are inspired by the confidence some of the artists showcased in the industry before going mainstream. Those are usually women that struggle with self-confidence in their everyday life. I feel as long as they're doing it for themselves its good, and also to promote a healthier lifestyle. But if its only for industry reasons, which is fine too, women want to be able to relate to a certain point, and feel inspired in genuine ways. We all evolve in the industry, its just better to do it by choice then to be forced.

Q. So what's next for you? What's your next project and what boss moves are you making in your industry?

A. Currently, I'm working on a mixtape which will be titled 3xotic's Box. I'm also working on a new album which will be out next year and will have a full storyline to tell some of the problems I've faced with no one knowing of my heartache durning the years... This album will show a different side of 3xotic. I'm also working on visuals to showcase the meaning of 3xotic and different faces of beauty. I'm currently producing and developing female artists. By next year I will be opening an artist development business. I also will be in a few web series's and short films.

3XOTIC

SNAP SHOTS

Email Your Snap Shots to
snapshots@sdmlive.com

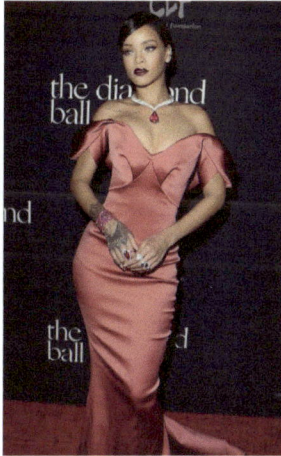

5DS PRODUCTIONS®
THE PRINT MEDIA CENTER.

PRINT

GET 10% OFF WITH CODE: SAVE10OFF

DIGITAL & PRESS RUN PRICE LIST

BUSINESS CARD 2x3.5 INCHES		TRIFOLD BROCHURE 8.5x11 INCHES		POSTCARDS 4x6 INCHES	
100	$10	250	$150	250	$50
500	$20	500	$180	500	$55
1000	$30	1000	$230	1000	$65
5000	$100	5000	$350	5000	$130
10000	$170	10000	$680	10000	$250

FLYERS - BROCHURES - BANNERS - BUSINESS CARDS - CD INSERTS CALENDARS - EVENT TICKETS - POSTCARDS - POSTERS YARD SIGNS - AND MUCH MORE

DIGITAL & PRESS RUN PRINTING

FAST TURN AROUND PRINTING

GET FREE SHIPPING ON ALL ORDERS

YOU SAVE MONEY WHEN YOU PRINT AT
WWW.THEPRINTMEDIACENTER.COM
24/7 ONLINE ORDERING. CALL US NOW 1.888.718.2999

COUPON CODE IS FOR A LIMITED TIME OFFER - FREE UPS SHIPPING ANYWHERE IN THE US

Urban Fiction, Spiritual, Motivation and more.

Order a book from Mocy Publishing today and receive FREE shipping.

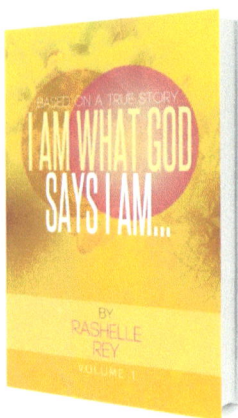

I Am What God Says I Am...
By Rashelle Rey

Item #: IAWGS29
Price: $9.99

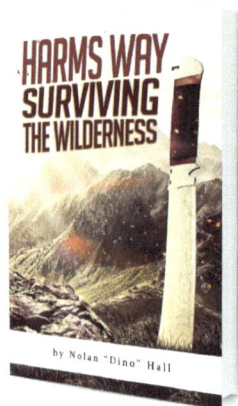

Harm's Way
By Nolan "Dino" Hall

Item #: HWS821
Price: $15.99

The Shadiest Mission Ever
By Cheraee C.

Item #: TSME28
Price: $12.99

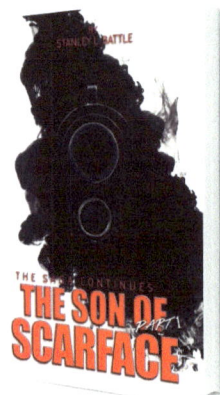

The Son Of Scarface – Part 1
By Stanley L. Battle

Item #: TSOS01
Price: $12.99

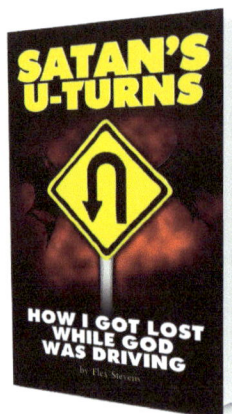

Satan's U-Turns
By Flex Stevens

Item #: SUT382
Price: $9.99

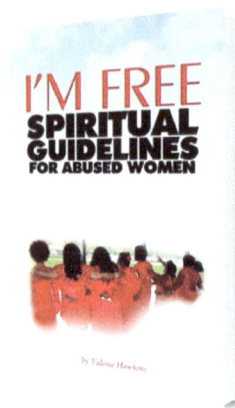

I'm Free
By Valerie Hawkins

Item #: IFTSG82
Price: $14.99

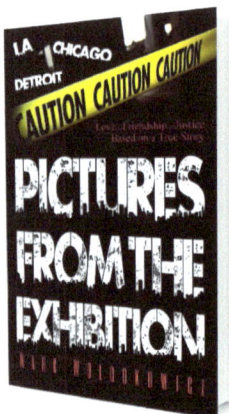

Pictures From The Exhibition
By Mark Wolodkowicz

Item #: PFAE292
Price: $15.99

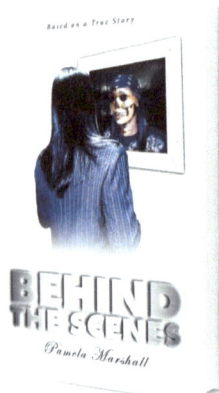

Behind The Scenes
By Pamela Marshall

Item #: BTS721
Price: $15.99

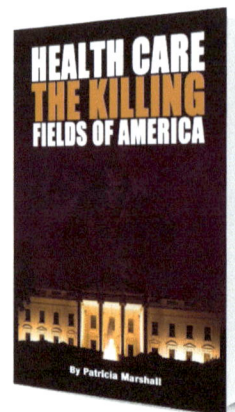

Health Care
By Patricia Marshall

Item #: HCTABF2
Price: $17.99

www.mocypublishing.com

order online and receive FREE shipping. Limit time offer.

REAL MUSIC. REAL ENTERTAINMENT.

S.D.M

ISSUE 3

ALSO
AUHMAZ!N
ISHMAELSOUL
MZ. PLATINUM
KID JAY

KOSTA
JUST HIT THE JACKPOT
WITH A NEW SMASH
HIT SINGLE "LOTTERY"

BIGG DAWG BLAST
LAUNCHES THE STREET
HITTA DJ'S MOVEMENT

Neisha Neshae

BRINGING IN 2016 ON STAGE
WITH THE KING OF R&B R-KELLY
& DROPPING A NEW MIXTAPE

PLUS MORE

THE RED CARPET EDITION
SUPERSTARS CAME WITH FASHION AT
THE SDM MAGAZINE RELEASE PARTY

US - $9.99 CANADA - $14.99

01 >

9 770317 847001

JANUARY 2016 No.3
WWW.SDMLIVE.COM

ORDER YOUR ISSUE FOR $9.99
Send money order plus $3.95 S&H to: Mocy Publishing, LLC
P.O. 35195 * Detroit, MI 48235

THE ALL NEW STYLE OF MAGAZINE-BOOKS